I0510588

Portraits

Book 4
in
Quick Tips by a Pro
Photographer
Series

by Julia Harwood

All Rights Reserved. No part of this publication
may be reproduced in any form or by any
means, including scanning, photocopying, or
otherwise without prior written permission of
the copyright holder. Copyright © 2012

Table of Contents

1. Special Thanks

I would like to make a special mention of a few people who without their support this series would not be possible. Firstly to my Proof Reader, Cathy Longley, no matter how sick you were you still managed to get these done, thank you so much. The to all my supporters on Pozible but most especially Angela Chan, as without her financial backing this project would not have been possible and finally to my wonderful husband Colin, who put up with me spending so many hours on the computer. I hope these help you on your photographic journey.

You can also follow me on my website at
Photography by Julia K Harwood
http://www.juliaharwood.com/

For all your gift needs
http://www.redbubble.com/people/juliakharwood/portfolio

To follow me on G+
http://plus.google.com/+JuliaHarwood

To follow on FB
http://m.facebook.com/Photography.by.Julia.K.Harwood

2. Portraits - Understanding Light

Apart from the people in portrait photography, the most important aspect is the light.

So lets look at lighting. There is short lighting, broad lighting, soft lighting, hard lighting, back-lighting, natural light, artificial light, flashes, reflectors and more. So lets explain a few of these to get you started.

The quality of light, is measured by the softness of the transitions from highlights to shadows, and so it is said to be soft if there is a nice gradual transition or hard if it is a sharp transition.

The softness or the hardness of the light is directly proportional to the size of your light source compared to your subject.

What this means is if you have a large light source like a flash inside a soft-box and it is fairly close to the person, then the light source is large in relation to the person and so will give you soft light, however if you move that same light further away it becomes smaller in relation to the person and so the light becomes harder.

This is an example of hard lighting, this one casts unwanted shadows.

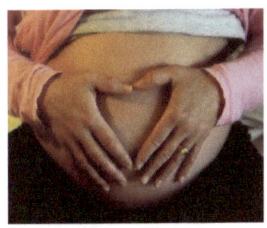

this one emphasizes the shape.

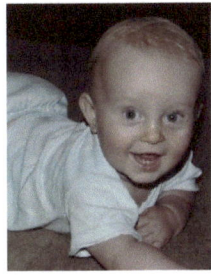

This is an example of soft lighting.

Short lighting is where the most light is falling on the smaller part of the face. The model will face towards where the light but so that the light only hits the smaller part of her face.

Broad lighting is the opposite in that the most light falls on a larger area of the face, so the model would look towards the light and the light will hit the larger area of the face.

This is short lighting see how only one cheek is lit. usually better for women.

This is broad lighting, the broad side of his face is lit. This makes him look bigger and more powerful.

Short lighting traditionally looks better on woman and broad lighting better for men as it tends to give a more powerful feel to the image. But when you are trying to portray a woman as powerful or the softer side of a man you can reverse this.

Back-lighting occurs when the light is behind your subject and we often find this in photos taken at the beach or at sunrise or sunset. You end up with a lovely scene and a black or very dark person with no detail in the subject.

If your subject is backlit you will need to add a fill flash or their face will be in deep shadow. You also need to watch for lens flare with a backlit image, so you can shadow the lens with your hand to stop the lens flare.

To use fill flash set you camera flash setting to -2 or -3. It is always best to add a fill flash with off camera flash or using a lite scoop, (I will explain these a bit later) but if you have neither of these as an option, then use the pop up flash on your camera. If you set the camera to Aperture Priority and then use the flash the camera in most instances will automatically use fill flash. Give it a try for your camera or check your manual.

In order to create softer light you need to move the subject closer to the light source, so that the light source is as large as possible in relation to the subject.

Another character of lighting is it's color or temperature. Light that is more towards the yellow or golden end of the spectrum is said to be warm, light that is more towards the blue part of the spectrum is described as cool or cold.
This becomes important when we want to add mood to our images, but also important in portrait

photography in that warm or golden light is the most flattering for the human face. This is why you will often hear people tell you that you should always shoot people images in the "golden hour"

The golden hour is the hour before sunset and the hour after sunrise when the sun is very low in the sky. This light has a lovely warm, golden hue and casts long soft shadows.

While we are on the subject of the temperature or hue of the light we need to mention white balance.

White balance determines what the camera reads as white, or grey.

Cameras are designed to average out the scene so that you have highlights and shadows with the largest area of the image falling into the grey area.

This is fine most of the time, however, there are certain situations you need to be aware of as the camera will not get it right on it's own. Most cameras have the ability for you to manually set white balance and you can also set them in post processing, especially if you shoot in RAW (more on that later)

So to take advantage of the golden hour, you need to turn off your auto white balance and use shady white balance or otherwise you can use a grey card to set the white balance.

As we said before, the camera automatically averages out the image you take to neutral grey, but if you are at the beach or taking a white wedding dress, as white is the dominant color, the camera will see this as grey and you will not end up with the look you are after.

So if you use a grey card, you are creating a reference point for the camera and to enable you to easily correct the white balance in post processing.

Some cameras allow you to take a shot with the grey card filling the frame and then manually set the white balance to this, which means a lot less fiddling around in post processing, so check your camera manual to see if your camera allows you to do this.

A grey card gives you a neutral tone so that when you import your photos to your software you can click on the grey area in the image to set your white balance and then you can add that setting to all your shots from that sitting. If you are taking photos for a while or moving to different areas you may need to do this a few times. As the light changes so does the white balance so do this every half hour.

To do this you set your white balance to custom and get someone to hold a grey card and take a sample shot, then use this image to set white balance in post processing.

You can also use a white piece of paper if you don't have a grey card.

You can buy grey cards online or from a camera shop or you can make your own.

An easy way to do this is open up Photoshop (or any image editor that can handle layers) and make a new document that's sized at 8.5" x 11"

and has a white background.
Make a new layer and fill it with black.
Reduce the opacity of that layer to 50%.
Print.
If your printer has a color profile, you may want to switch to that before printing for more accurate results. I did this with a cheap laser printer, however, and it worked really well. My gray card was uneven and pretty horrible in general, but I still ended up with better and more accurate color than the camera's automatic white balance. A proper gray card is definitely better, but when you need something quick you can get by with even this fairly inaccurate method.

Okay now that we have a bit of an overview of lighting and color temperature or balance we will move on to portraiture. I will cover flash a bit further on as this is a big subject all on it's own.

These are two setups using natural light from a window. Windows give us great light and we can add a sheer curtain to soften the light or use a reflector. Make sure the light is not streaming directly through the window or it will be too harsh.

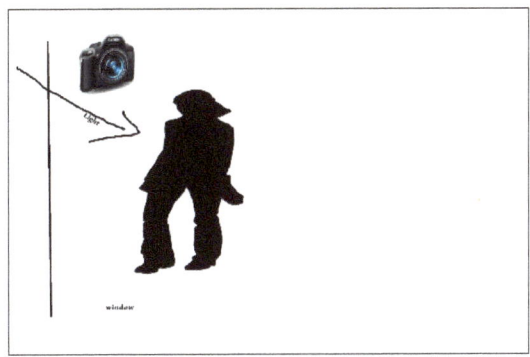

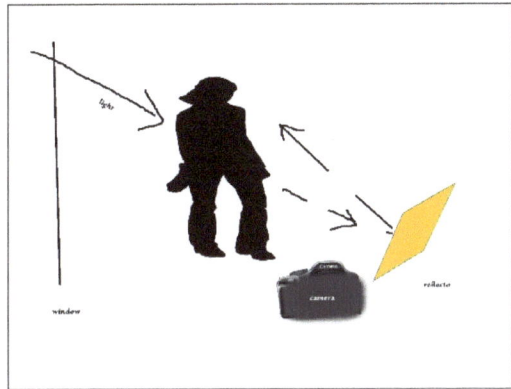

Great additional reading here

http://www.cambridgeincolour.com/tutorials/natural
-light-photography.htm

3. What Makes a Good Portrait?

First let us look at what makes a good photo.

A good photo has an interesting subject and a good story. This is also very true for portrait photography, especially if you want to capture the personality of your subject.

With portraiture as we already know lighting is also important and the ability to control it.

If there are eyes in the photo they need to be in sharp focus and preferably with a catch light in them. A catch light is a little reflection of light in the eye that gives the eye a lot more life.

We need to make the person feel good about themselves.

We need to be ready to catch those candid moments.

We need to understand what settings to use and what effect they have.

Finally we need to know how to edit them in post processing.

So let's head to the next chapter and learn how to tell a story with a portrait and how do we get the person to engage with us.

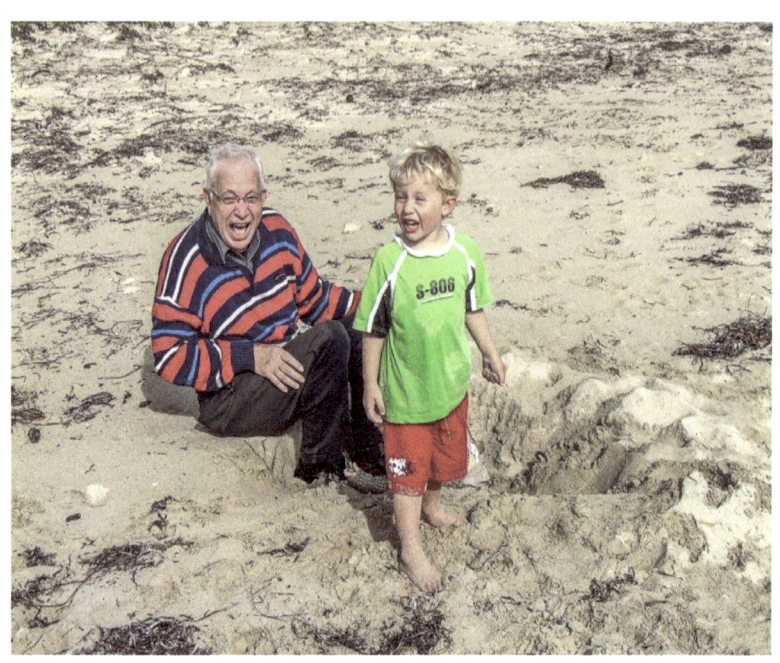

4. Engaging the Subject

A good way to engage you subject is to get them talking. Then they will forget about the camera and start to connect with you.

Here are some ideas to help you,

Tell me about your family, a favorite memory or some other positive thing.

When we connect we create relationship and curiosity.

Then we need to understand the smile. It always occurs in the eyes and the wrinkles appear at corner of eyes.

If we get the person to throw their head back and laugh, it will be fake and staged, but what happens afterwards when they laugh at themselves will be genuine.

So we wait for this moment – patience.

Then capture the moment.

To do this I recommend using more than one frame. Ideally set the camera to burst mode, if you aren't using flash, if you are then still take multiple shots. People blink and get quirky expressions, so the more we have to work with the better.

Here I find a remote shutter release button a real plus as I can interact with the person without them realising I am taking photos, not so easy when using flash.

You can also ask the person to smile with their eyes.

This gets rid of the big cheesy grin and the scrunched up eyes and it actually helps you quickly get beneath the masks.

Ask them to think of their happiest memory.

Remember to ask everyone to remove glasses and hats. Hats make the eye area very dark and glasses cause reflections, especially sunglasses.

If someone says, "But I always wear glasses" then, get them to move the arms of the glasses up a bit, so the glass is pointing down slightly. If you are still getting reflections then work out where the reflection is coming from and hold a black card between the person with the glasses and the object reflecting.

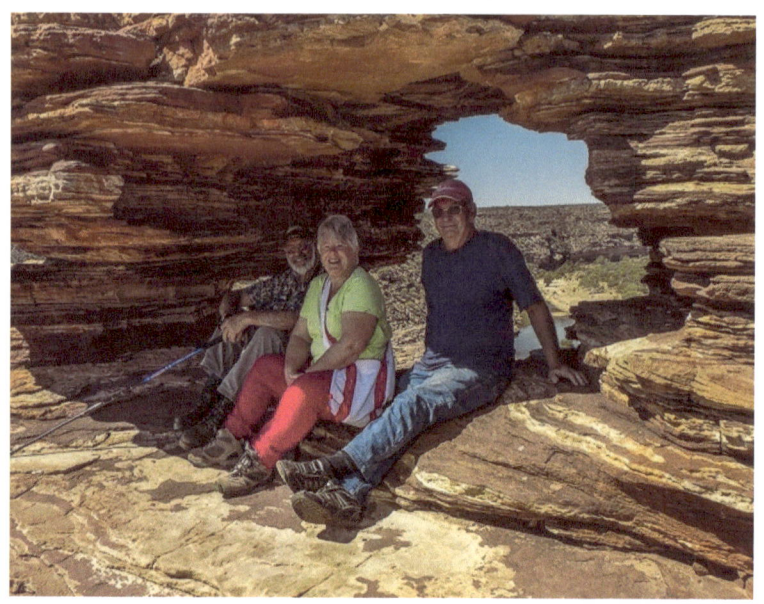

Here the glasses were left on and you can see how the reflections take away from the overall image.

5. Posing

People are often self conscious about how to stand, sit, or position their head, they are often self conscious about their appearance, so it is up to you to put them at ease and to show then how you want them. Don't just tell them, show them.

Firstly get the person to point their chin out, now lower the chin a little. This gets rid of extra chins. If a person has heavy eyes, shoot from a bit above so they need to look up a bit. Get then to tilt their head slightly one way or the other.

If the subject is particularly nervous or tense, get them to jump and you jump with them.

It helps them connect with you and most people find jumping amusing and are more relaxed afterwards. Get them to do the Toyota jump.

Another option is to get them to sit, most people instantly relax a bit when they are sitting down.

We normally face a man towards the camera as this accentuates his chest and arms, while a woman we turn their body away from the light but have then facing back towards it.

Whichever part is facing the camera appears larger, so if someone is self conscious about their tummy, face that away from the camera and then get them to turn their shoulders and head back.

Most women in particular, but men also these days want to look slimmer, so if you make sure there is a gap between their arms and their body this will help. Get them to put one hand on their waste and the other resting gently on top of this one, or similar, helps to create the look of a waist even if their isn't one.

Suggest they dress in darker colors and proper fitting clothes. often people hide behind oversize clothes, but this in fact makes them look bigger. If they have a top or dress on like this again use their hand placement to create the appearance of a waist.

Ask people what aspect of their appearance they like best and what is the worst.

This will give you an idea on how best to pose them to accentuate what they like about their appearance and minimize what they don't like about their appearance.

These are some very basic ideas, if you want to learn more there are some great articles online, one is http://photographyawesomesauce.com/20-things-i-wish-i-knew-about-photography-posing/

There are also apps you can get which are great to have on your phone to show the person what you are looking for.

At the end of the book there is some links to online classes that show you how to pose a client.

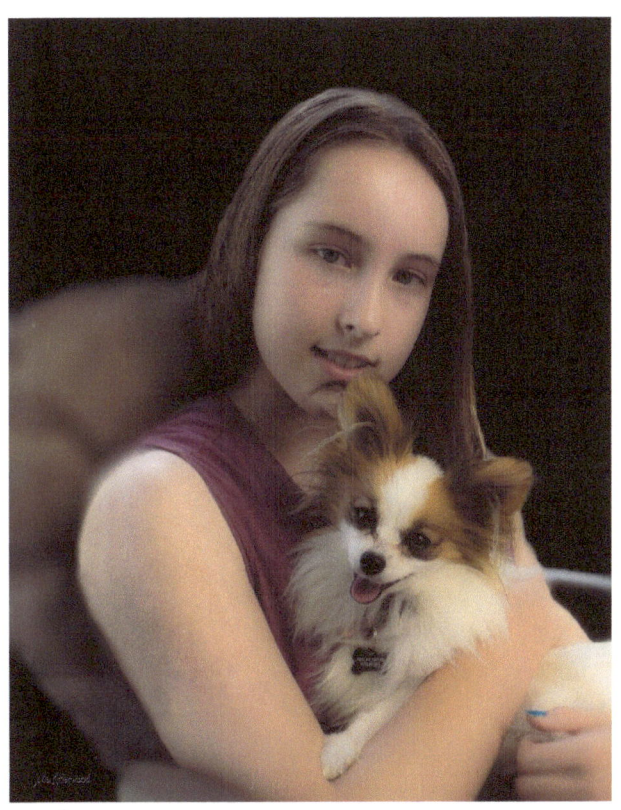

Often using a pet or a prop helps
to relax the person.

6. Setting

Now we need to look at the setting. The setting can help us tell the story. An environmental portrait is where you place them in an environment that tells a story about them. For example a truck driver in front of his truck or climbing up into the cab.

Backgrounds, these can make or break an image.

Here are some that work especially if you have a studio.

Light blue works well with Dark skin.

Red back ground makes blonde's look more brassy and bold.

Black for low key.

White for high key.

We can look for these in nature as well.

Look for complimentary colors, either between what the person is wearing and the background or between the people in a group.

These are some complimentary colors

Blue/orange

Purple/yellow

Green/red

If you look at a color wheel then any colors that are opposite each other on the wheel are complimentary.

If you are shooting at a time of day when the sun is acting as a harsh light, for example the middle of the day, you will want to look for shade, but be careful under trees that you don't get dappled light. Look for solid shade. If you can't find any and there is someone that can help you hold a diffuser between the person and the tree in the direction the light is coming from, this will minimise the dappled effect. A diffuser is the middle section of your reflector that the other bits zip on and off.

A great way to see where the shadows are falling on a subject is to squint at it. When we squint we are able to see the shade and light far better. It is really important that we control the shadows on people's faces.

If you are shooting in a crowded area, try to find a wall as a backdrop or frame the subject so that there is as little distraction as possible in the background. With other types of photography we can get low and shoot with the sky as the background but be careful with this as you don't want a shot looking up someone's nose or have their chins turn into double or triple ones. If possible you can get higher and shoot from above with them looking up at you. You can just sit them on the ground and you are then higher than them.

This brings us to camera angle

A camera pointing up shows respect but watch the nostrils.

Looking down on subject lets us know we don't need to be in awe of the subject, it creates a feeling of intimacy.

Straight on speaks of an honest portrayal of the subject.

Profile suggests an interesting character.

Unusual angles suggest quirkiness.

A portrait is all about the eyes. If the eyes are in the shot we want them to be in focus and have an interesting expression. It also really helps if they have a catch light in them.

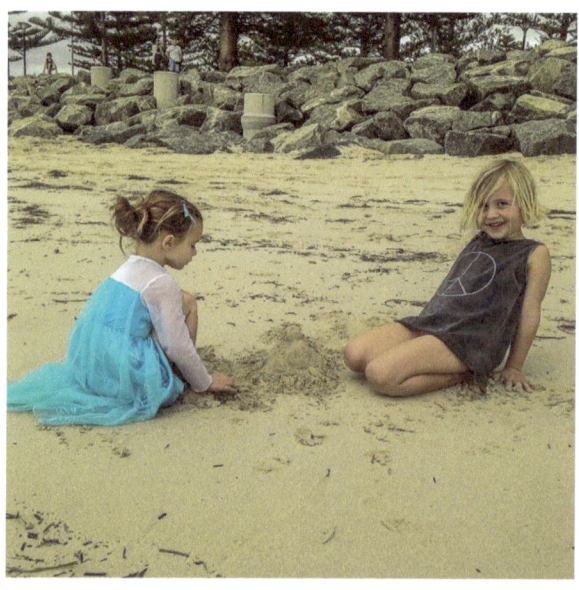

7. Aperture and Focal Length

Wherever you are shooting remember to use a wide aperture or a small f number, so that the background is blurred and the subject really stands out.

A note here though if you are shooting a group use at least f5.6 to make sure the group are all in focus. The bigger the group the larger the f stop as this gives you a larger depth of field.

You also need to decide if you want the whole face or person in focus or just the eyes. F5.6 at 100mm will have whole face in focus or f8 at 200mm (I will explain how this works in the book on macro)

While on focal length, for portraits we want a minimum of 50mm as any less and you will get exaggerated features such as big noses. I generally try to shoot between 50mm and 105mm. This is based on a 35mm camera, so you will need to adjust for a cropped sensor camera.

People always ask how to work it out for other cameras, so you look in your manual to see the crop factor of your camera and then multiply the focal length by that, however some manufacturers list the focal length on the lens as 35mm equivalent so check that first.

The best focal length is really quite a tricky one as people refer to the focal length ie 50mm, 85mm etc as being best for portraiture, but in reality the thing with portraiture is we don't want to negatively distort the features, this is actually determined by the distance between the model and the camera, not the actual focal length. It is actually a perspective issue and perspective is affected by distance not focal length, however they are usually bunched together as one.

So when you frame with a 50mm lens on a full frame camera the distance this puts you from the model is the absolute minimum distance you should be to take a portrait image, most photographers will tell you it is actually too close for a close up as you are invading the models personal space. So with a crop frame camera, 50mm is actually more like a 75 to 85mm on a full frame camera which is great as it puts you further away from the subject and able to get a nice image. *(Be aware that some camera manufactures list the focal length of the lens as 35mm equivalent).* Although for the purpose of teaching we say to use 50mm to 110mm, I personally never like to shoot closer than the 75mm equivalent of a 35mm camera. It allows me to frame the way I like to and gives a pleasing result, however that is my minimum, I more often shoot around 110mm, so the best idea is to experiment.

Take a series of images of a person at different focal lengths, but actually take them at different distances. For example use a wide angle but at 2 meters from the subject, then 1 m, then 1/2 m, do the same with a 50mm and then an 85mm and compare the images and work out what distance works best and then use the lens that gives you that distance. This will give you a better idea of what the best lens you would want to use for portraits.

But don't limit yourself. Experiment, a wider angle lens gives you a joker, comical look, great for a clown or funny man, longer lens can give a heavier more solid look, great for athletes, muscle-men, footballers. Standard 50mm in close and flattering, great for a baby or delicate lady.

If you are doing professional portrait shoots, especially weddings, always have a spare camera body, just in case one malfunctions.

Put your prime lens or your favourite portrait lens on one and then a zoom that covers 75mm and higher and have that on the spare body. This saves you time with not having to swap lenses as well as giving you options if you have problems with either camera or lenses.

Going back to aperture, if you want to just have the eyes in focus you will want an aperture of f1.8 to f2.4 and this will give you a beautifully blurred background.

The thing to watch here though is that you use an aperture which will give you enough depth of field to get the eyes in focus and sharp.

If the person is slightly side on you may find one eye falls out of the focal plain and out of focus, unless only one eye is in the shot it is best to avoid this, so make sure if the persons head is on a bit of an angle or they are slightly side on that you have a large enough depth of field to have them both in focus, usually f4.

We usually make our main focus the eye closest to the camera.

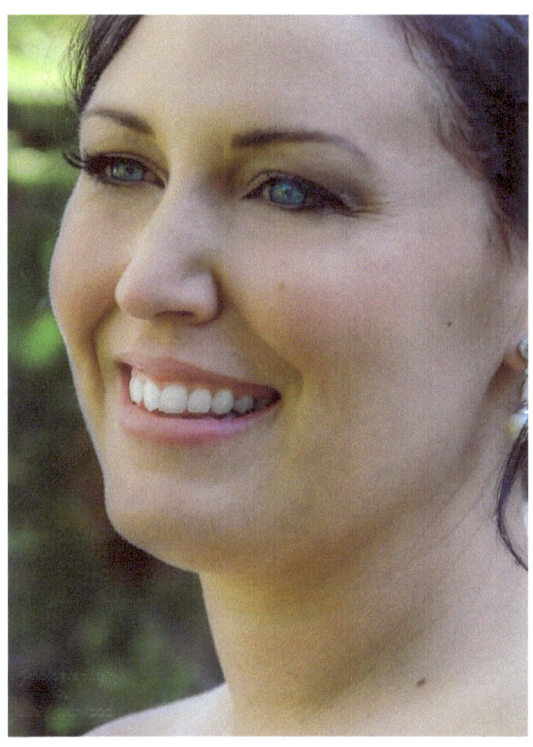

8. Shutter Speed

Avoiding subject-based blur is not quite so straightforward, but once you get a good feeling for your subjects and how quickly they move, shutter speed will start to become second nature. Obviously, the faster your subject is moving, the faster your shutter speed will need to be, but how fast?

Until you've developed that second nature, you can use the following guide to help you determine roughly how fast your shutter speed will need to be in order to avoid motion blur.

People sleeping 1/60
People posing 1/80
People and animals walking slowly 1/125

People and animals walking quickly 1/250
Bikes, people running, sporting events or kids playing 1/500

In portraiture aperture is how we control the background, but if we don't have a fast enough shutter speed then a blurry person will definitely ruin the image. So my first priority is to get a fast enough shutter speed for the situation, then see what the lowest aperture I can get that will work.

If I can't get a to the setting I want then I will increase the ISO only if I do not have the option of adding more light, my first choice is always to look to add more light.

We can add light through moving
the subject to a different location,
using shade, using reflectors and
using flash.

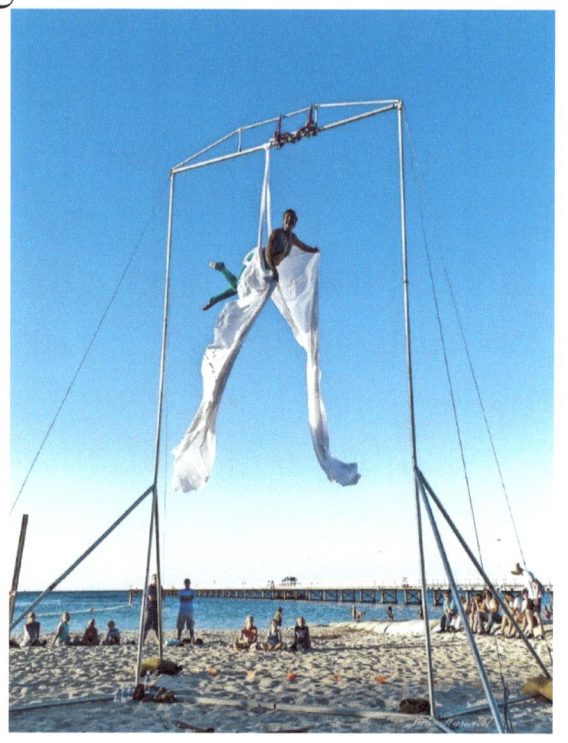

Fast shutter speed to freeze the
action. In this one I also used a
narrow aperture, or a high f number,
to get the surrounding in focus as
well.

9. Flash

Flash photography

Which brings us to flash photography.

Most people will tell you to never use on camera flash for portraits and here is why:

We end up with deer in the headlight look to the eyes and a general flatness to the image.
However, there are ways we can use our on camera flash and not give this effect.

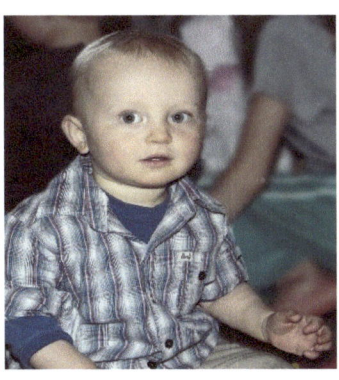

In general for portraiture we want as even a light as possible, but if we use light to sculpt the image with shadows we can create some very dramatic images, but before we get to this we need to know how to create a well lit even image with flash.

Remember light illuminates, shadows define.

If your flash isn't giving you enough light, then move it in closer to the subject. There is a formulae for working out amounts called the "Inverse Square Law", but to simplify it, putting it at half the original distance will make it four times as powerful. Even with TTL modes this is important to know as TTL will only compensate to 100%, if you still don't have enough light then you have to make manual adjustments.

Be aware though that the closer you move your light to the subject the more quickly the light falls off, so if you want to light more of the scene you need to move the flash further away, while at the same time increasing the power of the flash.

Moving a light closer to a person will not only make that light more powerful, it will also make it softer as it becomes a larger light source. The larger the light source the softer the light. Inversely the further away you move it the harder the light is as the light source becomes smaller in relation to the person or object. So it is important to soften the light with a softbox, shooting through an umbrella or into a light scoop.

If you don't have these you can improvise by using some sheer fabric between the subject and the light, bounce the light off the wall or roof if it's not too high. Do this only if the wall or ceiling is white or you will get a color cast in the final image.

Why do we bounce flash?
It softens the light. The larger the light source in relation to the subject, the softer the light and therefore less shadows. The smaller the light source in relation to the subject the harder the light and therefore the harder the edges of the shadow.

You can buy a lite scoop here http://www.litegenius.com/new/ or have a go at making your own.

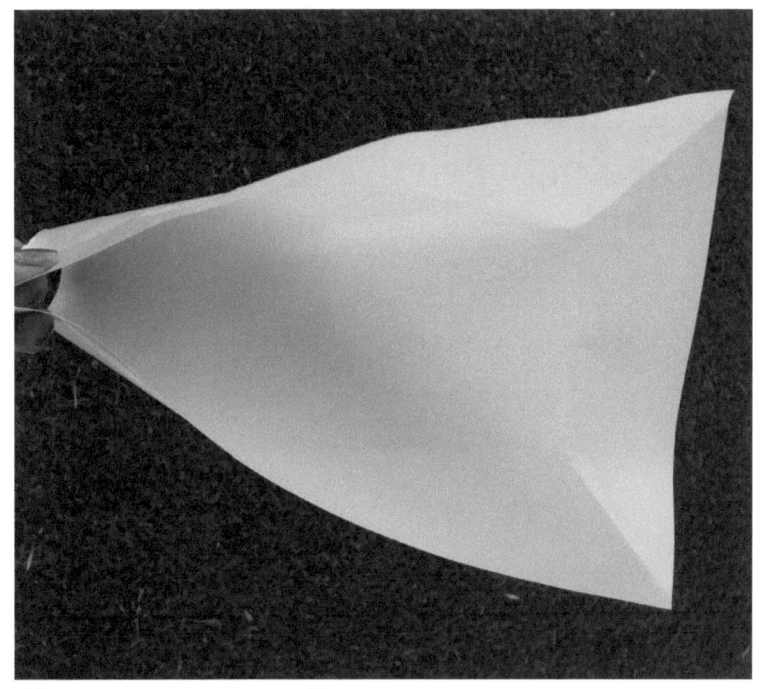

This was my first one.

If you only have one flash, and want to light your subject separate to your background and avoid shadows falling on the background or backdrop then you need to move your subject as far away from the background as possible.

To make this work you need the distance of your subject to the background to be larger than the distance between the light and your subject.

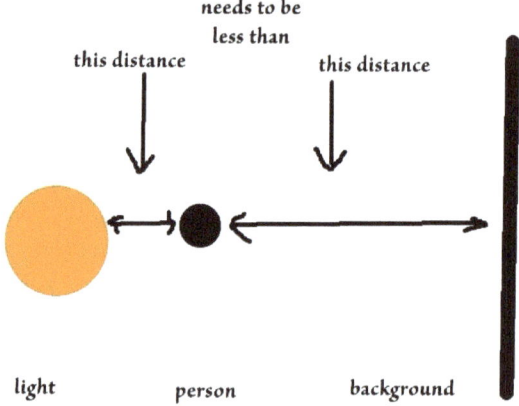

To avoid the persons shadow falling on the background or backdrop

needs to be less than

this distance

this distance

light

person

background

Another way to control the background is to add a light or flash between the backdrop and the subject.

Have the light pointing up and slightly towards the back of the subject. This adds back-lighting to the subject and creates a greater contrast between the background and the subject. Make sure the camera can't actually see the light.

A technical note:
You will often hear people or articles refer to guide numbers. The Guide number is the distance your flash can reach for a particular setting. So if you divide the guide number (for a specific ISO, as you change the ISO the guide number will also change) by the aperture you are shooting at, you will get the distance your flash can cover.

When you light a group of people who are standing one slightly behind the other, or if you are lighting a group from the side, then you shouldn't put your light too close to them, or the ones farthest from the light source line may end up being under-exposed. To avoid this, move the light source further away, so that the distance between the group members is small compared to the distance between the light source and them. The further the subject to the light source the less fall-off of the light.

This can be tricky as every time we double the distance that the flash is away from the subject we need to increase the power 4 times.

So it is often a juggling act of getting the right amount of light verses having the light source too close and risking the far side of the group not being lit properly. Unless of course you have two light sources as then you can set one up each side.

A good way to see how light works is this:

Light or flash closer *increases* the strength of the light but *decreases* the spread of the light which then *increases* the softness of the light.

Moving light closer increased strength but decreases spread therefore creates a softer light.

Light or flash further away *decreases* the <u>strength</u> of the light but *increases* the <u>spread</u> of the light which then *increases* the <u>hardness</u> of the light.

Smaller light in relation to subject = harder light but increased spread(good for groups)

Remember we can use a soft-box or diffuser or umbrella or light scoop to soften the light.

Situation	Solution
Want softer light	move light closer
Need more light strength	move light closer
Need less spread	move light closer
Want harder light	move light further away
Want less light strength	move light further away
want more light spread (groups)	move light further away
Want soft light and more light to keep ISO low and shutter speed up, but want more spread to cover a group	Move light closer and add a second light to the other side, be careful not to have falloff in the middle of group. if you do add reflector or bounce flash.

A great way to see shadows is to squint. If you squint at a picture or a scene you will see the shadows much more clearly. Do this as you set up your lights so that you can see any shadows as they appear.

The other trick is to set up one light at a time then add another light or reflector to fill in shadow areas.

Aperture controls the amount of light from the flash and shutter speed controls the ambient light. As long as you are below your cameras sync speed, generally around 1/250 second then it won't affect the flash. You can look up your camera sync speed online or in your manual.

So if you want to *increase* the light that the camera sees from the flash then use a wider aperture, or lower f number. If you want to *decrease* the light from the flash then use a smaller aperture or a higher f number.

If you want less exposure in the background increase the shutter speed, but don't go over the sync speed of your camera or you will end up with black portions in the image.

If you want to increase the exposure in the background then you lower the shutter speed.

So the things that affect the flash are aperture , distance to subject, strength of the actual flash and whether you are bouncing the flash or not.

These are some starting settings for flash photography. You will need to experiment with your own camera and flash and then write down the basic settings for your gear.

These settings will just give you somewhere to start.

Flash photography settings for indoors.
ISO 400 1/200 f4.5
ISO 200 1/200 f5.6
TTL (Through the lens)

Use diffuser on flash or a Light scoop (picture)
You can buy them online or make your own.

Check your manual for what settings you can use TTL. For some cameras you have to be in Aperture priority mode.

These are examples of the correct settings for my camera.
Subject 2m away 75mm 1/200 f4.5 ISO 100 flash bounced in umbrella and set at 1/2

Subject 3m away 75mm 1/100 f3.6 ISO 100 flash shoot through umbrella and set at 1 (full power)

Remember the most important part is getting the person in focus and lit how you want them, so get this right first, then set your shutter speed for the background, but don't go below the minimum settings for a still shot (1/80) or you will end up with blurred people.

These are a couple of lighting setups to help you.

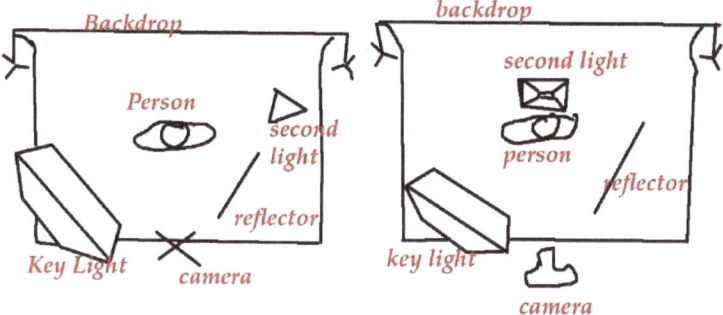

10. Silhouettes

We want to capture the subjects side-on
Subjects with a clear profile such as people, animals and trees work best. Make sure that the subject is positioned to reveal its most recognizable features.
With a person or an animal this will usually mean shooting them side-on. The other important consideration is to frame the subject so that the entire outline is against a bright background. If necessary, shoot from a lower viewpoint to get the full profile of the subject, and to avoid the bottom of the subject getting lost.

Spot meter for background. Spot metering is where you point your camera at the brightest area and then set your exposure for this if using manual, if not then use the ev/ef lock button on the back of the camera.

Shoot into light, but hide sun behind object or wait till it is just below the horizon.

Have a clean background, get low if necessary to show the whole silhouette.

Remember, don't chase perfection to the point of missing the shot. We as humans are not perfect and a character shot is usually better than a technically perfect shot that looks posed.

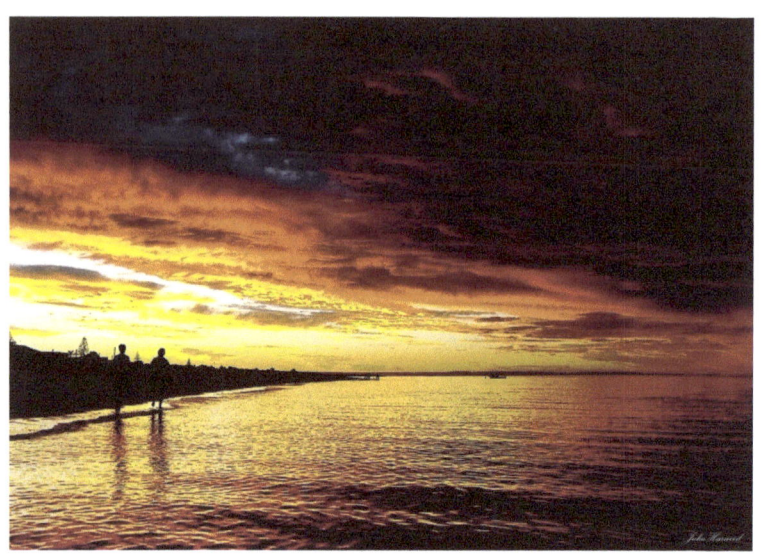

11. Post Processing

Due to the fact that this is a quick tips ebook, I am not going to go into indepth post processing, but I do want to just let you know that if you are able to use layers in your post processing then there is an easy way to give people a bit of a glamor look. Open your image in post processing and duplicate the layer, now you can use unsharp or clarity and reduce the sharpness of the image, this softens the skin and reduces wrinkles. You then add a layer mask to this layer and invert it , then paint on it with a white brush in the areas that you want to be soft.

For those without a layers option, you can select the face and neck, then deselect the eyes, ears, mouth and tip of nose, make sure you feather the selection, then use either unsharp, decrease clarity or even reduce noise to soften this area.

These are some online tutorials to help you more.

http://photodoto.com/retouching-photoshop-tutorials/

12. Extra Resources

Here is a great article on portraiture.
http://www.digital-photo-secrets.com/tip/3314/5-camera-setting-tips-for-shooting-great-portraits/
http://digital-photography-school.com/10-ways-to-take-stunning-portraits/

Great article on portraiture posing
http://photographyawesomesauce.com/20-things-i-wish-i-knew-about-photography-posing/

Craftsy Photography Courses

Beautiful Bridal Portraits
http://craftsy.me/1CYiJPo

Portraits with on camera speedlight
http://craftsy.me/1Aefe7C

Off camera Flash photography
http://craftsy.me/1BwFQ5I

FREE: Professional Family Portraits
http://craftsy.me/1AZuK7T

Wedding- posing the family
http://craftsy.me/1EzS6QE

Studio Portrait Lighting
http://craftsy.me/1MGs03Y

You can also get the other books in this series:
http://www.amazon.com/s?ie=UTF8&page=1&rh=n%3A133140011%2Cp_27%3AJulia%20Harwood

Book 1 - Starting Out
Book 2 - Making Photography Easy
Book 3 - Low Light Photography

Also bookmark this page so that you will now when my Quick Tips on other subjects come out. Next one will be Photographing Animals.

13. Cheat Sheet

Portrait cheat sheet

On arrival
Camera set to burst mode
Scene mode set to portrait mode or you can use AP, aperture priority
Tripod, spare camera, batteries all charged, spare SD card, Remote shutter
On arrival, walk around and look for place light is going to be best, preferably coming from slightly in front and off to the side.
Set Camera and lights up.
Check off camera flash is ON.
Chat to people, help them relax as you put them where you want them.
Ask everyone to take off hats and glasses
Check for shadows.
Be creative.
If using tripod, Turn image stabilization OFF!!!

Portraits.
Tell me about your family, a favorite memory or some other positive thing
1. Connect - relationship and curiosity
2. Wait for the moment - patience. Capture the moment
3. Experiment -Which lens? don't limit yourself. A wider angle lens gives you a joker, comical look, great for a clown or funny man, longer lens can give a heavier more solid look, great for athletes, musclemen, footballers.
Standard 50mm in close and flattering, great for a baby or delicate lady.
4. Use more than one frame.
5. Understand the smile. It always occurs in the eyes and the wrinkles appear at corner of eyes.
Get person to throw their head back and laugh, this will be fake and staged, but what happens afterwards when they laugh at themselves will be genuine.

Flash

1/2 the distance and it increases flash strength by 4

double the distance and it reduces flash strength by 4

You can only go to 100% then you need to add another light (or change location)

If you don't want background shadow less distance between light and person compared to person and background.

Or, place a light between person and background facing up and slightly forward.

To soften light, move it closer.

For harder light, move it further away.

For more intense light move it closer.

For weaker light move it further away.

For great spread of light, less fall off, move light further away.

For less spread, light falls off quickly, move light closer.

Aperture controls the flash light.

Shutter speed controls the background or ambient light.

Diffuse the flash or light, soft box, lite scoop, umbrellas, reflectors or bounce.

www.ingramcontent.com/pod-product-compliance
Lightning Source LLC
Chambersburg PA
CBHW040839180526
45159CB00001B/241